BITTERNESS

RESOURCES FOR BIBLICAL LIVING

Lou Priolo, series editor

BITTERNESS

THE ROOT THAT POLLUTES

LOU PRIOLO

P&R PUBLISHING

P.O. BOX 817 • PHILLIPSBURG • NEW JERSEY 08865-0817

The contents of this book have been adapted from several of the author's previous books: primarily *The Complete Husband* (P&R, 2017), *The Heart of Anger* (Calvary Press, 1998, with permission), and *Picking Up the Pieces* (P&R, 2012). The author has also relied heavily upon Jay Adams's books *How to Overcome Evil* (P&R, 1977, 2010) and *From Forgiven to Forgiving* (Calvary Press, 1994).

Unless otherwise indicated, Scripture quotations are from the NEW AMERICAN STANDARD BIBLE®. Copyright © 1960, 1962, 1963, 1968, 1971, 1972, 1973, 1975, 1977, 1995 by The Lockman Foundation. Used by permission.

Italics within Scripture quotations indicate emphasis added.

Printed in the United States of America

Library of Congress Cataloging-in-Publication Data

Priolo, Lou.
  Bitterness : the root that pollutes / Lou Priolo.
     p. cm. — (Resources for biblical living)
  Includes bibliographical references.
  ISBN 978-1-59638-130-8 (pbk.)
  1. Resentment. 2. Forgiveness. 3. Emotions—Religious aspects—
Christianity. I. Title.
  BV4627.R37P75 2008
  241'.3—dc22
                    2008032367

FRED CAME HOME from a late night at the office. After scarfing down his reheated supper, he went into the bathroom to brush his teeth. The moment he opened the vanity drawer and spied the tube of toothpaste that his wife had squashed *in the middle* (for the umpteenth time), he flew into a rage. Slamming the drawer closed and flailing his arms, he began verbally accosting Wilma in a rather loud and irritated tone of voice.

"That woman! She's always squeezing the toothpaste tube in the middle. I've asked her a thousand times to roll it up from the end. But does she listen to me? Never! I might as well talk to the toothpaste tube itself rather than ask her to do something for me. She is the most stubborn, pigheaded woman I've ever met. How would she like it if I ignored her incessant requests? She wouldn't like that one bit."

At this point, Fred stopped speaking out loud but continued to muse over the toothpaste tube as he internally plotted to get even.

"I'll teach her a lesson. She hates it when anyone in the family forgets to replace the cap on the toothpaste tube. So, I'm going to leave it off. Tomorrow morning when she comes in here to brush her teeth, she'll be furious that I 'forgot' to replace the cap, and that will ruin her whole morning. And maybe, if I'm lucky, the toothpaste will harden overnight in the neck of the tube, and when she goes to squeeze some out, she won't be able to. And just maybe, she'll look into the neck of the tube as she tries to firmly squeeze it, and a little pellet of hardened toothpaste will pop out of the tube and hit her smack between the eyes!"

Now let me ask you, is a squashed tube of toothpaste worth expending all of that emotional energy? Hardly! What kind of response does a tube of toothpaste that has been repeatedly squashed in the middle deserve? If the toothpaste incident can't be overlooked altogether, then (at the very most) about all the time, effort, and thought that one should devote to it is something along these lines:

"Oh, look at that! She squashed the toothpaste tube in the middle again. Maybe we ought to invest in individual tubes."

When we exert inordinate amounts of emotional energy over such trivial disappointments, it's a good indication we may be bitter.

What Is Bitterness?

One of the biblical words for *bitterness* literally describes the bitter taste of certain foods and drinks. The verb translated "to be bitter" means "to cut" or "to prick." You may think of bitterness as an internal, self-inflicting wound, and so it is. But the Bible says that this resentful, unforgiving attitude will cut and prick others as well.

Bitterness is the result of not forgiving others. If you are bitter at someone, it means that you haven't truly forgiven that person. To put it another way, bitterness is the result of responding improperly (unbiblically) to an offense.

The Scripture likens bitterness to a root:

See to it that no one comes short of the grace of God; that no root of bitterness springing up causes trouble, and by it many be defiled. (Heb. 12:15)

Roots have to be planted. So let me ask you, "What do you suppose is the seed that when planted in the soil of our hearts sprouts into a root of bitterness?"

Generally speaking, it is *a hurt*. When someone hurts you,[1] it is as if that person dropped a seed of bitterness onto the soil of your heart. At that point, you can choose to respond in two ways. Either you can reach down and pluck up the seed by forgiving your offender, or you can begin to cultivate the seed by reviewing the hurt over and over again in your mind. Bitterness is the result of dwelling too long on a hurt. Again, it is the indication that one has not truly forgiven an offender (cf. Matt. 18:34–35).

Veronica's best friend, Betty, had been planning a sleepover for all the girls in the youth group. All summer long, the party was the topic of discussion. Everyone was going to be there. Three days before the sleepover, Veronica found out that some old family friends were coming over the weekend of the party. Although Betty's party had been scheduled months before, Veronica's father wanted her to drop her "silly little party plans" and stay at home with their houseguests. Veronica knew that all the popular people would be at the sleepover, in addition to all her friends. Plus, she made a commitment to the party long before she even knew about her father's plans. Veronica's father insisted that she stay home. He has just dropped a seed of hurt onto the soil of her heart.

Veronica's seed of hurt could be easily transformed into a root of bitterness:

---

1. The hurt can be real or imagined; it makes no difference. The result is the same. If you do not deal with it biblically you will become bitter. If I hurt you as a result of my sin and you choose not to overlook it or cover it in love (Prov. 17:9; 1 Peter 4:8), you must follow Luke 17:3 and pursue me with the intent of granting me forgiveness, and I must repent. If you get your feelings hurt as a result of something I did that was not a sin, you must repent of your unbiblical thinking that caused you to be "offended" at something that was not a sin.

Veronica's Internal Thoughts	Cultivation of Veronica's Bitterness
"I can't believe he's doing this to me! I've been planning to go to this sleepover all summer long."	Veronica presses the seed an inch or two into the soil of her heart.
"He's so selfish. All he thinks about is what he wants."	Veronica covers the seed with more soil.
"He is never willing to let me have fun if he thinks his precious plans might be upset."	Veronica aerates the soil.
"Why did I get stuck with a father like him?"	Veronica waters the seed.
"He's such a loser!"	Veronica fertilizes her hurt and it starts to sprout.
"I can't wait until I can get out of here. Then nobody will be able to spoil my fun."	Veronica weeds her little sprout, and its roots grow deeper.
"He can't do this to me. I'm going to give him a taste of his own medicine. I am going to embarrass him so badly that he'll wish that he had sent me to the sleepover in a limousine."	Veronica puts the finishing touches on the greenhouse that houses her stinkweed and begins charging people admission to see it.

Veronica allowed her hurt feelings to paralyze her from taking the appropriate action (such as respectfully obeying and perhaps appealing graciously to her father), replayed his "offense" over and over again in her mind, and consequently became embittered against him.

Evidences of Bitterness

What are the indications that we have become bitter toward another?[2] In my almost twenty-five years of counseling I have come across a few possible indicators of bitter-

2. If you are bitter, you probably need little verification. The Bible says, "The heart knows its own bitterness" (Prov. 14:10).

ness. I offer them for your consideration. With how many of these can you personally identify? Begin by thinking about the people closest to you.

Difficulty in resolving conflicts. Trying to resolve conflicts with someone you are unwilling to forgive is like trying to build a skyscraper without first laying a solid foundation. The bitterness will doom the project before it gets off the ground.

Acts of vengeance. Whether it takes the form of a back-biting verbal comment to another, a spiteful remark to the offender's face, or some kind of physical altercation, taking one's own vengeance is a sure sign of unforgiveness.

Withdrawal. When we give our offenders "the silent treatment" or "the cold shoulder," we are likewise being vindictive. We are saying (essentially), "Look, I've tried to tell you over and over again how much it bugs me when you do (don't do) that. But you just don't get it. So, the only thing I know to do to show you how much you've hurt me is to give you a little taste of your own medicine. When I think you have an inkling of how much you've hurt me—perhaps in a day or two—I'll start talking to you again!"

Outbursts of anger. As we saw with Fred, bitterness tempts us to overreact emotionally. When we are bitter, we don't see each new offense on a clean slate that is relatively easy to forgive, but rather as one more item on a long and growing list of similar offenses under a common heading (e.g., "Hurtful Things She Has Said to Me Over the Years").

Biting sarcasm. Ironic intonations, snide remarks, mean-spirited joking, caustic comments, scornful replies, and other such forms of sarcasm are often generated in a resentful heart.

Condescending communication. Speaking to your offender as though he were a child or an inferior is not only a possible indication of bitterness, but contrary to Philippians 2:3b, "but with humility of mind regard one another as more important than yourselves."

Criticism. A critical, condemnatory, judgmental attitude may also indicate a problem with resentment. Frequently, a retaliatory motive is at the heart of a censorious spirit.

Suspicion and distrust. When bitterness causes a breakdown in communication (as it commonly does), the parties become suspicious of each other. Small "offenses" that typically would be dismissed with a "He didn't mean anything by that—I've done it myself a hundred times" or an "Oh, he's just having a bad day" kind of thought are then interpreted with less charitable motives.

Intolerance. Similarly, bitterness disposes us to not put up (forbear; cf. Eph. 4:2) with our offender's idiosyncratic (nonsinful) behavior. Resentment makes mountains out of molehills.

Hypersensitivity. Treating a pinprick as though it were a knife through one's heart may likewise be indicative of an unforgiving spirit. Proud individuals are especially prone to fall into this snare.[3] "You haven't offended 'any ole per-

---

3. Proud people are much more likely to harbor bitterness than the humble. Humility compares the small temporal offenses that it must forgive against the enormous eternal offenses for which it has been forgiven by God (see Matt. 18:21–35).

son,' you've offended 'me.' And my anger is not so easily propitiated."

Impatience. Patience involves being able to keep a biblical perspective about our troubles by not magnifying a tolerable trial so that it appears to our minds as an intolerable one. Bitterness causes us to lose this biblical perspective. It magnifies forgivable offenses so that they seem unforgivable in our minds. And it tempts us to resort to unbiblical means of delivering ourselves from the trial rather than waiting on God to work through our peacemaking attempts to resolve the conflict biblically.

Disrespect. If the person at whom we are bitter is an authority figure, our contempt for that person will eventually make its way out of our hearts and into our mouths in the form of irreverence.

Rebellion against authority. Rebellion hardly ever occurs apart from bitterness. It begins with a seed of hurt, then sprouts into bitterness, matures into stubbornness (insubordination), and then develops into contumacy.

Misuse of authority. When bitterness toward a subordinate is in the heart of an authority, it can produce a domineering, dictatorial, or tyrannical attitude that demands needless exactions of obedience.

Depression. After continually running around a track, you and I would ultimately deplete our supplies of energy and become physically exhausted. Our bodily strength would be zapped from our bodies. The same principle holds true on an emotional level. It requires vast amounts of emotional energy to maintain a grudge. After several laps around the unforgiveness track (several days of bitterness), most of us will have depleted (zapped) our emotional energy and become emotionally exhausted (i.e., depressed).

Doubts regarding salvation. Jesus, after teaching His disciples to pray "forgive us our debts, as we also have forgiven our debtors," said to them, "If you forgive others for their transgressions, your heavenly Father will also forgive you. But if you do not forgive others, then your Father will not forgive your transgressions" (Matt. 6:12, 14–15).[4] Our unwillingness to forgive an offender in light of all that we have been forgiven in Christ *should* give us pause to consider whether we are truly in the faith (cf. Matt. 18:21–35).

Remembering with great specificity the details of an offense. Bitterness eulogizes the particulars. It is actually possible, by replaying the offense over and over again in our minds, to confabulate (unconsciously replace facts with fiction) details that never actually occurred.

Regardless of how you've been hurt, as a Christian who is committed to pleasing God, you really have no choice but to forgive your offenders of any sins they have committed against you.

Bible Basics about Forgiveness

Most of the principles that follow are based on Luke 17:3–10. Other passages have been cited where applicable:

---

4. Space will not allow me to unpack the other "spiritual consequences" of bitterness, such as hindrance to prayer (Ps. 66:18), grieving (Eph. 4:30) and quenching the Spirit (1 Thess. 5:19), and inability to fully love God (1 John 4:20).

"Be on your guard! If your brother sins, rebuke him; and if he repents, forgive him. And if he sins against you seven times a day, and returns to you seven times, saying, 'I repent,' forgive him."

The apostles said to the Lord, "Increase our faith!" And the Lord said, "If you had faith like a mustard seed, you would say to this mulberry tree, 'Be uprooted and be planted in the sea'; and it would obey you.

"Which of you, having a slave plowing or tending sheep, will say to him when he has come in from the field, 'Come immediately and sit down to eat'? But will he not say to him, 'Prepare something for me to eat, and properly clothe yourself and serve me while I eat and drink; and afterward you may eat and drink'? He does not thank the slave because he did the things which were commanded, does he? So you too, when you do all the things which are commanded you, say, 'We are unworthy slaves; we have done only that which we ought to have done.' "

Forgiveness is to be granted only if a sin has been committed against you. Jesus said, "If your brother sins . . . ." He didn't say, "If he doesn't give you what you want," "If he lets you down," "If he hurts your feelings," or "If he profoundly disappoints you." Your brother may do any and all of these things in the process of sinning, but he is not in need of your forgiveness unless he *sins* against you.

If what your brother has done to upset you is not a sin, it may be appropriate for you to talk with him about the matter at some point, but not before your thinking about the "offense" has changed. In other words, it is not your offender who must repent, but you must repent of your unbiblical thinking that took offense at something that God did not.

Sometimes the offended party must initiate forgiveness. If you cannot overlook the transgression (Prov. 19:11) or cover it in love (1 Peter 4:8), you are obligated as a Christian to go to a brother who has sinned against you and "rebuke him." Sometimes, we must go to our sinning brother and tell him about his sin with the intention of being able to grant him forgiveness.

"But *he* sinned against me! Why does his sin obligate me to go to him? Didn't Jesus say somewhere that he is supposed to come to me before he brings his gift to the altar?"

He did. In Matthew 5:23, Jesus tells us to seek forgiveness from those whom we have offended. In that passage the *offending* party is told to go.

But we are looking at Luke 17, which says the *offended* party should go. Since you, as the offended party, are the one who has knowledge of the wrong, you are to go. The one who knows about the offense is the one who goes. Perhaps your offender doesn't know about his sin, or maybe he doesn't want to seek reconciliation. Or, as happens rather frequently, it could be that there is a misperception on someone's part that requires a discussion to clear up the issue. It might even be discovered that no real sin was actually committed.

Forgiveness is costly. When you forgive someone, it costs you something that is tremendously expensive. It costs you the *price* of the *offense* that you forgive![5]

But more importantly, what it costs you is minutiae compared to what it cost the Lord Jesus to forgive you of your sins. That is why unforgiveness is such a heinous crime in the eyes of Him who is the judge of the whole earth. In the parable

5. One of my graduate school professors used to speak of forgiveness as being analogous to giving an expensive gift. Basically, what we do when we forgive someone is to pick up his offense, place it in a colorful box, tie a pretty ribbon around the box, place a lovely bow on top, and then hand it back to the person whom we are forgiving.

of the unforgiving servant, Jesus referred to the protagonist as "wicked," who after being forgiven an incalculable debt refused to forgive a much smaller debt.

> "You *wicked* slave, I forgave you all that debt because you pleaded with me. Should you not also have had mercy on your fellow slave, in the same way that I had mercy on you?" And his lord, moved with anger, handed him over to the torturers until he should repay all that was owed him. (Matt. 18:32–34)

In light of how much you have been forgiven by God, for you not to forgive those who offend you is *wickedness*. It doesn't matter how much the offense that you are struggling to forgive hurt you; by comparison to your offenses against God and the hurt you put His Son through, the offense that hurt you is minutiae! It is even more wicked for you as a Christian not to forgive than for your pagan friends who have not experienced firsthand so great a forgiveness as you have, and who have not been given the power to forgive through the Holy Spirit.

Never forget: the debt that you owe to God for your sins is *humanly incalculable* and *absolutely unpayable*. You will *never* be able to repay God for the trillions of dollars' worth of debt your sin has incurred in the bank of heaven. It is a debt that has been totally paid for by the death of Christ on the cross. To Him you are now eternally indebted!

Almighty God—the Creator and Sustainer of the universe—is the Judge who sent His Son to die in your place so that He could slam the gavel on His bench and say, "The penalty has been paid, your debt has been forgiven, you are free to go." What ingratitude it is for Christians not to forgive their offenders! Dare we slap Him in the face by refusing to forgive those petty little offenses in light of all He's done for us?

Forgiveness is fundamentally a promise. In his insightful book *From Forgiven to Forgiving,* Jay Adams explains:

> When God forgives, He goes on record. He says so. He declares, "I will not remember your sins" (Isa. 43:25; see also Jer. 31:34). Isn't that wonderful? When He forgives, God lets us know that He will no longer hold our sins against us. If forgiveness were merely an emotional experience, we would not know that we were forgiven. But praise God, we do, because forgiveness is a process at the end of which God declares that the matter of sin has been dealt with once for all.
>
> Now what is that declaration? What does God do when He goes on record saying that our sins are forgiven? God makes a promise. Forgiveness is not a feeling; forgiveness is a *promise!*[6]

When you forgive, you are promising to no longer hold your offender's trespasses against him. You are also promising to impute your forgiveness to him (much like Christ imputed His righteousness to you when you became a Christian). The dictionary defines the verb *impute* as follows: 1) "to charge with the fault or responsibility for"; 2) "to attribute or credit."[7] When you promise not to impute your offender's trespasses against him, you are promising to no longer charge him for what he has done. This means you are not going to allow yourself to dwell on the offense. You will refuse to cultivate those seeds of hurt, but rather will immediately

6. Jay E. Adams, *From Forgiven to Forgiving* (Amityville, NY: Calvary Press, 1994), 11–12.

7. *American Heritage Dictionary of the English Language,* 3rd ed. (New York: Houghton Mifflin, 1992).

pluck them out of the soil of your heart. You will relinquish all "rights"[8] to get even.

When you promise to impute your forgiveness, you credit your offender's account with your forgiveness, much like Christ credited your heavenly account with His righteousness. You make every effort to think well of him, to pray for him, and to speak well of him, if possible. This promise, to some extent, can be made in the form of a personal commitment in your heart even if your offender does not acknowledge his sins to you. This is what is sometimes referred to as "forgiving someone in your heart" (see Mark 11:25).

If he does acknowledge his sins and asks for your forgiveness, you will make this promise to him as you verbally grant him forgiveness. In such cases, you will be making him two additional promises. The "not remembering his sins" concept is an implicit promise to never bring up the offense to him again. If you have forgiven him, there is no need to discuss it again. Similar sins that he may commit in the future may require new confrontations. In addition, when you verbally grant someone forgiveness, you are promising not to tell anyone else about the offense.[9]

Forgiveness is not the same as trust. If someone sins against you, it is incumbent upon you as a Christian to forgive that person as you have been forgiven by God in Christ (cf. Matt. 18:21–35). However, it is incumbent upon that person to earn back the trust he lost as a result of his sin. Forgiveness should be immediate. Trust may take time (see Matt. 25:14–31; Luke 16:10–12). But please be warned: to withhold trust after it has

---

8. As a Christian, you really don't have such a right as personal vengeance (Rom. 12:17–21).

9. If other individuals have a biblical need to know about the offense, you can lovingly urge the offender to confess to all necessary parties so that you will not be obligated to disclose it to anyone.

been earned is unloving. The Bible says that "love believes all things" (1 Cor. 13:7). This means that if we love someone, in the absence of hard evidence to the contrary, we will put the best possible interpretation on what he does—in this case, believing that the fruit of repentance he has brought forth is genuine. And whether or not you are able to quickly trust your offender, you must always trust God to work through him and to protect you from danger.

Forgiveness does not focus on secondary causes but on the sovereignty of God. Joseph had to *learn* to trust in God's sovereignty. We sometimes think that when Joseph was sold into slavery by his brothers (the secondary causes of his trial), he somehow said to them, "Don't worry, guys, you mean this for evil, but someday you'll see that God means it for good," after which he broke out into a joyful chorus of Romans 8:28 ("We know that God causes all things to work together for good"). But what really happened was disclosed years later by his brothers:

> Then they said to one another, "Truly we are guilty concerning our brother, because *we saw the distress of his soul when he pleaded with us,* yet we would not listen; therefore this distress has come upon us." (Gen. 42:21)

In the final analysis, God could have prevented the offenses that have tempted us to bitterness—but He didn't. Forgiveness focuses not on the offender's sin but on how God (in His wisdom and goodness) may be using the offense for His glory. We should assume that God is more concerned about our response to the offense than the offense itself.[10]

10. Sometimes an offense is God's way of revealing to us a need in our offender's life so that we might pray for (or even minister to) him.

This leads us to another matter: bitterness toward God. I have devoted several pages to this topic in Appendix A. If you think that you may be bitter at God, let me urge you to turn there now.

Forgiveness involves an act of the will—not the emotions. If your offender repents, you must forgive him—quickly.[11] Jesus phrased this concept in such a way as to make it clear that (in the absence of evidence to the contrary) you have to take your offender at his word and grant him forgiveness. Look again at Luke 17:4:

> And if he sins against you seven times a day, and returns to you seven times, saying, "I repent," forgive him.

Even if it is the seventh time in one day that he has asked you to do so, you are to forgive him.[12] Jesus does not give you very much time to get your feelings in line *before* you forgive. You are to do it as an act of your will in obedience to God. Your feelings will follow. If you wait until your feelings change before you forgive, you may never obey the Lord's command.

In the verses that follow (5–10), the disciples had a hard time with Christ's teaching on this subject. Their response to

11. If your offender does not repent, to prevent bitterness you will have to apply Mark 11:25. Jesus said, "Whenever you stand praying, forgive, if you have anything against anyone." You must, in other words, somehow forgive your offender "in your heart." I have prayed something like this on occasion: "Lord, You know what my offender did and how much it hurt. You also know that what I really feel like doing is to give him a taste of his own medicine. But I know that to retaliate in kind is wrong. So, in obedience to You, as an act of my will, I impute my forgiveness to his account just as You imputed Your forgiveness to mine."

12. This is not to say that *for his sake* you cannot call into question (urge him to examine) the sincerity of his repentance before you grant him forgiveness. Indeed, when there is *hard evidence* to refute his claim of repentance, it would be unloving not to call him into question (by asking him to explain the incongruence between his claim and the evidence).

Him was an incredulous "Increase our faith." They thought they needed more faith in order to obey this teaching. Through a parable, Christ instructed them that it was not more faith they needed, but rather more faithfulness. The slave in the story was not being asked to do something he was incapable of doing, despite how exhausted he might have *felt* after returning to his master's house from a long day's work. Preparing the evening meal was something he was expected to do. It was not optional. Neither was it something for which he would be receiving time-and-a-half pay for working overtime. He couldn't even expect to receive special commendation. It was his job! Forgiveness is a part of your job description, too. Like any job, some responsibilities are easier and more enjoyable than others. Some you feel like doing; others you do whether or not you feel like doing them.

"But what if *after* I forgive him, I begin to have feelings of resentment toward him? I'll feel like such a hypocrite!"[13]

You will not feel that way if you learn to think biblically about the matter. After granting forgiveness, remind yourself that you made a promise to your offender. Don't let that seed of hurt develop into a root of bitterness by dwelling on it. Pray for him and put your mind into a Philippians 4:8 thought pattern: "Whatever things are true, whatever things are noble, whatever things are just, whatever things are pure, whatever things are lovely, whatever things are of good report, if there is any virtue and if there is anything praiseworthy—meditate on these things" (NKJV).

Rather than reviewing hurtful mental images from the past, or laying vindictive plans for the future (seeing the

---

13. Keep in mind that it is *not* hypocrisy to feel one thing and do another (something totally contrary to your feelings). Chances are you did that first thing this morning when you got out of bed. It is hypocrisy to profess one thing and do another. For you to tell your friends how much you enjoy getting up in the morning, if you don't, would be hypocrisy.

face of your offender on a dartboard, or on a baseball you are about to pulverize with your "Louisville Slugger"), picture his face with the words "I've forgiven you" boldly imprinted across the image. Put your imagination to work on Philippians 4:8 (or other relevant passages of Scripture). You may be surprised at how much better you will feel, as well as how quickly you will forget, once you truly forgive. Forgetting is the result of forgiving, not the means of it. It is the final step of the process, not the first one.

The Key to Transforming Your Feelings

My wife, Kim, and I had been married for less than a year. It was Saturday morning, and she was hurt by something I had done. No matter how I tried, I couldn't seem to resolve the conflict with words alone. After about twenty or thirty minutes, I decided to do something radical. I wrote her a note explaining that I was going to the store, making it clear to her that I would be back momentarily. I left the note on the kitchen table and went out to buy her some flowers. I distinctly remember the drive to the flower shop. I was hurt and very angry with Kim as I pleaded with the Lord: "Please help her to see how unreasonable she's being." I was rehearsing some of the conflict in my mind, partially cultivating that root of bitterness; yet I was in the process of showing her love. My mind was struggling with cursing her, but my body was in the process of blessing her. I was, as an act of my will and in direct contradiction to my emotions, trying to overcome (what I perceived as) her evil with good. "Do not be overcome by evil, but overcome evil with good" (Rom. 12:21).

As I continued driving to the store, trying to fight bitterness, my emotions continued to torment me. I walked into the store resolutely determined to "fight back" biblically, still struggling with bitter feelings. And then it happened. The moment I picked up those flowers, my entire thought pattern and emotional response immediately and radically changed.

"I can't wait to see the expression on her face when I give her these flowers," I thought. "As soon as she sees them, she's going to melt. She won't be able to stay upset with me now. This is going to knock her socks off. She'll not be able to resist any longer!"

The drive home was quite different from the drive to the flower shop. Excitement and anticipation grew as I rehearsed what I was going to say to her (cf. Prov. 15:28). My heart began to fill with loving feelings that had eluded me all morning. I was actually looking forward to the ensuing conversation.

I walked through the door with an entirely different attitude from when I had left. As I presented the flowers to her, she was obviously moved. I knew that the flowers were not going to solve the problem but would probably open the door for us to resolve the conflict biblically. When Kim realized that I was going to show her love in the face of her being less than loving to me, she softened. Within ten minutes, the conflict was brought to a total, biblical resolution.

Understanding and applying Romans 12:17–21 is the key to moving from forensic forgiveness to "feeling" forgiveness.[14]

Never pay back evil for evil to anyone. Respect what is right in the sight of all men. If possible, so far as it depends on you, be at peace with all men. Never take your own revenge, beloved, but leave room for the wrath of God, for it is written, "Vengeance is Mine, I will repay," says the Lord. "But if your enemy

14. I am grateful to Jay Adams, who taught me the following concepts. They may be found (more fully expounded) in his book *How to Overcome Evil* (Nutley, NJ: P&R Publishing, 1977).

is hungry, feed him, and if he is thirsty, give him a drink; for in so doing you will heap burning coals on his head." Do not be overcome by evil, but overcome evil with good.

I'd like to focus your attention on the last verse for another moment. This is the summary statement of the paragraph. It is the river into which the preceding verses converge. "Do not be overcome by evil, but overcome evil with good." This imperative contains two difficult commands that will need explanation. The first injunction is: "Do not be overcome by evil." That is, "You may not lose in your personal battles against evil." Think about that. You are actually commanded not to lose this particular battle you are fighting. Conversely, if you *do* lose in your fight against evil, you have sinned.

Before I explain further, let me call your attention to the fact that this entire paragraph is filled with terminology of war. Although some believe that Christianity is a pacifistic religion, the Bible is filled with battle terminology instructing the believer to have the mind-set of a soldier. The passage before you is a prime example of this.

In verse 17, you are warned against the improper use of weapons and briefed on the importance of developing a battle plan. Verse 18 stresses the importance of peace (the antithesis and desired result of war). Verse 19 cautions you not to take personal vengeance and offers guidance on the do's and don'ts of retaliation. Verse 20 provides you with instruction on how to destroy your enemy (with coals of fire). Verse 21 twice contains the wartime term for *conquer* (*overcome*).

Now, who is the enemy spoken of in this passage? The enemy is evil—evil people and the evil that people do. So, here you are fighting evil, and the Lord tells you that you may not lose. That is, you may not allow your offender's sin to overcome you.

You may not retreat.

You may not surrender.

You may not give up.

You may not throw in the towel.

You may not wimp out.

You may not allow his evil to prevail against you.

You may not allow his sin against you to provoke you to sin.

Symptoms of Battle Fatigue

How many battles have you lost? Do you have any symptoms of battle fatigue? Here are a few common indications that you may have been overcome by evil:

☐ Thoughts of resentment toward your offender.

☐ Telling yourself things like, "He'll never change," or "I just can't put up with this person any longer."

☐ Unnecessarily limiting the scope of your communication because of unsuccessful attempts to resolve conflicts with him in the past.

☐ Allowing anger to keep you from confronting him biblically.

☐ Allowing yourself to become sinfully angry, anxious, or depressed about the ways in which he has hurt you.

☐ Allowing your "hurt feelings" to keep you from fulfilling your biblical responsibilities—especially toward the person at whom you are bitter.

☐ Resorting to sinful, retaliatory actions such as:
    ☐ abusive speech
    ☐ gossip
    ☐ name-calling
    ☐ pouting

- [ ] quarreling
- [ ] slander
- [ ] sulking
- [ ] temper tantrums
- [ ] threats
- [ ] withdrawal

If you have even one symptom of battle fatigue, you almost certainly have lost a battle by allowing the other person's sin to overcome you. You have responded to sin with sin and are in violation of Romans 12:21a: "Do not be overcome with (defeated by) evil."

Fighting to Win

As difficult as that may be for you to believe, the second command in this verse may tempt you to greater incredulity, for it is even harder to obey.[15] The second injunction, Romans 12:21b, is: "Overcome (conquer) evil with good." What Paul is essentially saying is, "You may not accept anything less than victory in your personal battles against evil." That is, you must win the war. Paul is saying, "You may not cease from pursuing your opponent with good until you win the war." You are to pursue the enemy until the enemy gives in. There is no place in this verse for stalemates, no place for standoffs, no impasses, no mutual (bilateral) disarmament, no deadlock, no cease-fire before the victory. You are not to be conquered, but you are to conquer. The question is not "How long can I hold out in the face of his attacks?" but rather, "How can I use the resources God has given me to fight with to defeat the foe?"

15. It is possible only through the enabling of the Holy Spirit, who indwells exclusively those who have put their trust in the Lord Jesus Christ for the eternal salvation of their souls. Only a true Christian can continue to love in the face of unrequited love. Only a Christian is able continually to show 1 Corinthians 13 love, which "bears all things, believes all things, hopes all things, [and] endures all things" in the face of evil.

This second command not only requires you to win the battle but also defines the means you are to use to secure the victory. You see, God is interested not only in whether you win or lose but in how you play the game (or fight the battle, in this case). Means are very important to God. The only means whereby you may defeat the enemy—indeed, can defeat the enemy—is by using good. Your weapons must be only those armaments that can be considered good in God's eyes according to the Scriptures. With this state-of-the-art artillery that God has provided, you can fight back harder than your opponent. Blow for blow, good is more powerful than evil.

"This retaliation doesn't sound very Christian to me. Besides, Romans 12:17–19 seems to forbid all forms of retaliation."

Let's back up and unpack the entire passage.

Never pay back *evil for evil* to anyone. (Rom. 12:17a)

This passage actually doesn't forbid *all* forms of retaliation. It forbids retaliating *in kind*. You may not retaliate in kind—that is, with evil. You may fight back, but you may fight back only with good. The ammunition you load in your firearm must be bullets that are biblically certified as "good." Your motive is not to hurt, but to bless your offender with goodness until goodness overtakes his sin and motivates him to repent (cf. Rom. 2:4).

Consider two more New Testament passages that contradict the passive approach.

Not returning evil for evil, or insult for insult, *but giving a blessing instead*; for you were called for the very purpose that you might inherit a blessing. (1 Peter 3:9)

Rather than returning evil for evil or insult for insult, you are to (actively) give a blessing in return. This is hardly a passive response.

> See that no one repays another with evil for evil, but always *seek after* that which is good for one another and for all people. (1 Thess. 5:15)

The term *seek after* in this verse may also rightly be interpreted *persecute*, as it is in Romans 12:14: "Bless those who persecute you; bless and do not curse." The passage might well be understood this way: "See that no one repays another with evil for evil, but always *persecute* one another (and all men) with good." This is hardly the response of a doormat.

"But what about turning the other cheek? What you're saying seems to contradict the words of Christ."

Not at all. Matthew 5:39 ("But I say to you, do not resist an evil person; but whoever slaps you on your right cheek, turn the other to him also.") is more of an aggressive command than you might think. It is actually an offensive weapon designed to win the war against evil.

> The false interpretation of turning the other cheek that equates that action with defeatism, doormatism ("all I can do is lie here and invite you to wipe your muddy boots on me"), pacifism or non-aggression must be exposed for what it is—a non-Christian misrepresentation of the truth. Everywhere the Bible teaches that the Christian must aggressively fight against evil and overcome it.
>
> The Christian can no more take a passive attitude toward evil than his Lord did. He came into this world to take captivity captive. He came to destroy the works of the evil one and render him powerless (Hebrews 2:14). He "disarmed rulers and authorities, and made a public display of them" (Colos-

sians 2:15). There was nothing passive about the cross. The cross was *active*. He was sacrificing Himself for the sins of His people to free them from the chains of sin and the devil. Why then should they willingly submit to these shackles once more?

The Bible teaches the violent, not passive, overthrow of the enemy. He must be smashed to smithereens, demolished, utterly devastated. No quarter may be given. His power and place are to be destroyed. The Christian position is the most violent and aggressive one of all.[16]

Remember that the enemy is not (necessarily) your enemy. It is rather the evil that your offender regularly inflicts on you. It's not that you are to "do your enemy in," but you are to "do in the evil he does." Allow me to use a more vivid metaphor:

When your enemy shoots his popgun at you, you may fire back with your pepper spray.

If he pulls out a water pistol, you can hit him back with a douse of your flamethrower.

If he aims his peashooter at your forehead, you engage your missile launcher.

If he brandishes a slingshot, you pick up your bazooka.

Should he resort to a SCUD missile, you launch your Patriot missile at him.

The next imperative in the Romans 12 passage requires you to draw up a battle plan:

Plan ahead to do what is right in the sight of all men. (v. 17, my translation)

16. Adams, *How to Overcome Evil*, 22–23.

Few translations bring out the literal meaning of the verb that begins this command. It's actually a participle that literally means "to think of beforehand." God is saying that you must plan your next response to evil before the next battle. That's right. You must anticipate beforehand (cf. Prov. 15:28) how you are going to respond to the conflict so that when you find yourself in the heat of the battle, you will not respond to evil in kind, but rather respond to it with good. This is how soldiers are prepared for battle in basic training. They are drilled on how to fight before the battle so that in the heat of combat, they will respond automatically in the right way.

Do you know exactly how you are going to respond to your offender the next time he sins against you? Have you prepared your arsenal? Have you cleaned and loaded your weapons? Have you practiced fighting with them? If not, you'll likely pick up the first (familiar but sinful) weapon at hand when the bullets start to fly (and thus be overcome by his evil rather than overcoming his evil with good).

The next command has two clauses—one is conditional, the other unconditional.

> If possible, so far as it depends on you, be at peace with all men. (Rom. 12:18)

The first stipulation is the *conditional* one, "*If possible*...be at peace with all men" (believers and unbelievers). It is not always possible for Christians to be at peace with unbelievers—even in marriage (cf. 1 Cor. 7:15). But there is no reason why two *believers* cannot learn how to be at peace with one another. Indeed, they are commanded to "make every effort to keep the unity of the Spirit through the bond of peace" (Eph. 4:3 NIV).

The second clause is *unconditional*: "*so far as it depends on you*, be at peace with all men." You must "pursue peace

29

with all men" (Heb. 12:14) *regardless* of their response to you. Your obedience to God does not depend on the response of others. Your love for your neighbor (or enemy) should not be conditional (in that it is not predicated on his love for you). Regardless of your offender's willingness to be at peace with you, *you* should be willing (initiating and pursuing) to be at peace with him—especially if he is a fellow believer.

Now, if your offender is not at peace with you, don't assume first of all that it is because he is not at peace with God. It's possible that the reason you are not at peace with him is because of some things that "depend on you." Let me suggest in the form of three questions some reasons why your offender may not be at peace with you.

1. Have I *provoked* him to evil? Your offender's evil against you may, in part, be a sinful response to an evil that you have first committed against him. While he is not thereby exonerated, you are required to seek his forgiveness for any sin you may have committed that provoked him to evil in the first place.

2. Have I *protracted* (aggravated) his evil by a sinful response in return? Is it possible that rather than responding with good to your offender's sin, you responded in kind (perhaps with even more evil than he inflicted against you) and that such a sinful response on your part has contributed greatly to the lack of peace between you?

3. Have I *prolonged* the problem by not dealing with it quickly? Conflicts between believers are to be resolved expeditiously. "Therefore if you are presenting your offering at the altar, and there remember that your brother has something against you, leave your offering there before the altar and go; first be reconciled to your brother, and then come and present your offering" (Matt. 5:23–24). The longer you wait to resolve them, the more bitterness and suspicion can take root and fester.

The next command in our text is found in Romans 12:19.

Never take your own revenge, beloved, but leave room for the wrath of God, for it is written, "Vengeance is Mine, I will repay," says the Lord.

Have you ever wondered why the Bible forbids you from taking your own revenge? Why does God insist on doing it for you? There are at least two reasons. First, He has not given you (or any one person) the *authority* to take personal vengeance on anyone. What Paul is addressing in this passage, you will remember, is personal conflicts against evil people, or the evil that people do. In the next chapter (13) of Romans, Paul deals with the official, corporate, or governmental right of God-ordained authorities to execute vengeance: "for it is a minister of God, an *avenger* who brings *wrath* on the one who practices evil" (Rom. 13:4). Haven't you seen such wording (*avenger* and *wrath*) before? "Never take your own *revenge*, beloved, but leave room for the *wrath* of God, for it is written, '*Vengeance* is Mine, I will repay,' says the Lord" (Rom. 12:19).[17]

You see, vengeance is not for you to take personally (individually). It is a judicial issue, not a personal one. Ultimately, God is the One who will (directly or indirectly) right all wrongs. Vengeance is lawlessness because it doesn't recognize the lawful and righteous execution of God's judgment that He will bring about in His time. In other words, vengeance amounts to being impatient with God. You must remember that wrongs can't always be righted right away (cf. 1 Tim. 5:24).

17. It is sometimes good to remember the promise of Galatians 6:7 in our struggles against bitterness: "God is not mocked. For whatever a man sows, this he will also reap." In some form or other, the person who offends us is already suffering the consequences of his sin. And don't forget the lesson of Psalm 73: The apparent prosperity of the wicked is only apparent.

Vengeance does not belong to you. It belongs to God. " 'Vengeance is Mine, I will repay,' says the Lord." If God were to say to you, "This is My crown," would you walk up to Him and take it off His head?

"Of course not, that would be stealing (not to mention foolish)!"

Well, what do you think you're doing every time you take your own revenge? You're *stealing* from God. Don't do it. He didn't give you such authority.

The second reason you are forbidden to execute your own vengeance is that you really don't have the *ability* to do so. You don't have the ability because you don't have all the facts necessary to make the proper judgment.

Take a look at 1 Corinthians 4:5:

> Therefore do not go on passing judgment before the time, but wait until the Lord comes who will both bring to light the things *hidden in the darkness* and disclose the *motives of men's hearts*; and then each man's praise will come to him from God.

There are things hidden from you that only the Lord knows. Suppose your enemy (or offender) is suffering from a physical disorder that makes it easier for him to become angry. While this would not exonerate him from culpability, it would require a bit more mercy than you would be disposed to give him by not having all the facts. Or, suppose he has done the same thing to twelve other people this month and deserves a more serious judgment than you would think to give him. Additionally, you do not know his motives. They, likewise, might be better or worse than you realize. Only God knows what they are. "Man looks at the outward appearance, but the LORD looks at the heart" (1 Sam. 16:7). The amount of vengeance required by God's justice is predicated on His knowledge of men's motives, to which you have not been given total access. Keep this in mind the next time you're tempted to be vindictive.

We're now ready to unveil the ultimate weapon for dealing with those who fight against us with evil (Rom. 12:20).

> But if your enemy is hungry, feed him, and if he is thirsty, give him a drink; for in so doing you will heap burning coals upon his head.

Jesus tells us to love our enemies (Matt. 5:44). Paul (and Solomon; cf. Prov. 25:21–22) tells us *how* to do it. We love people by meeting their needs.[18] This is the ultimate weapon to use against those who habitually offend us. If they are hungry, feed them. If they are thirsty, give them a drink. If they have needs, take a look at your resources to see if you can somehow provide for them. Let me say again that overcoming evil with good is also the best way to overcome residual feelings of bitterness you may still have for your offender after you have forgiven him in your heart.

"OK, I understand the marching orders. But tell me, what about those coals of fire? What are they?"

Since virtually everything I've written in this section I've "learned and received and heard" from my friend and mentor (and fishing buddy) Jay E. Adams, I'm going to let him answer that question in his own words. *"The coals are your good deeds heaped on him."*

> Remember, Paul has warfare in mind. In his day, they didn't have flame throwers, but they knew that fire was an effective weapon. If you could get coals (of smokeless undetectable charcoal, as the word here indicates) on your enemy's head,

---

18. We love our enemies by meeting their needs but not necessarily by fulfilling their desires.

33

you would effectively put him out of business as an enemy. You would subdue and overcome him.

Picture your troops holding your heights above the pass. Secretly you have heated large beds of charcoal to white heat. As the unsuspecting enemy passes directly beneath, you shovel them on his head. You have him! You've defeated him! He is rendered powerless, helpless! You've stopped him in his tracks. That is the picture.[19]

Perhaps the person at whom you are bitter is someone you consider to be a real enemy—or close to it. If so, the problem you may be having with what I am suggesting is that for one reason or another you don't have regular access to him. There are two appendixes in the back of this booklet ("Appendix B: Loving Another from Afar" and "Appendix C: Loving 'in Absentia' Worksheet") that may help you better put what I have said so far into practice.

Now that you have a basic understanding of your marching orders, let me set up a battlefield scenario so you can see for yourself how to apply this passage. The examples employed in the following marriage illustration are intended only to give you a basic idea of how to implement the passage we have just unpacked.

Natasha informs her husband Boris that she needs a new widget for the kitchen. He disagrees that it's something that is really necessary, but after listening to her appeal, he concedes to the purchase. The only stipulation he places on her is that she not spend more than $25 on the widget.

First conflict: Natasha comes home from the store with the most expensive version of the widget on the market. It cost $63.50. She just hit Boris in the neck with a stinging pelt from her peashooter.

19. Adams, *How to Overcome Evil*, 104.

Now, what is he going to do? Is he going to unleash his pet rattlesnake on her with a string of unbiblical utterances? No. This time Boris is going to do what he's been planning on doing since the last time Natasha flagrantly ignored his instructions. He is going to pull out his slingshot and carefully load it with *good*. After forcing himself to say something nice about the widget, which he still believes is superfluous, he is going to calmly set her down and gently ask her if she remembered his instructions. After all, the Bible says (in 2 Tim. 2:24–25) that "the Lord's bond-servant must not be quarrelsome, but be kind to all, able to teach, patient when wronged, with gentleness correcting those who are in opposition," and such a biblical response is a good one.

Second conflict: Before he can finish the first sentence of his well-thought-out argument, Natasha becomes highly defensive. As he tries again, she raises her voice, accuses him of being "cheap," and stands up crying, "You don't love me! You never buy me anything I ask for without making me feel miserable about it! I need it, and I'm not going to take it back!" Then she stomps out of the room and storms off to the bedroom, slamming the door so hard that three pictures and a plate fly off the wall. She has bruised his head with a .45-caliber slug. What is he going to do now?

Boris calmly (and prayerfully) goes back to his biblical arsenal and pulls out his .357 Magnum. He has already anticipated (planned ahead for) his next move. So, it's no big deal. He has practiced it numerous times in his mind. He decided that while she was sulking in the bedroom, fuming at him, he was going to do the dishes for her. After that, he plans on vacuuming the floor. Then, he will make Natasha a cup of her favorite tea and bring it up to her on a tray, along with a fresh flower he's just cut from the yard placed in her favorite bud vase. "Yes!" he says to himself. "This will do her in. She'll never be able to resist." The anticipation grows. As he begins to do those loving things for her, his feelings continue to improve. He notices a spring in his step and a song starting to come from his mouth. "Victory in Jesus, my Savior forever . . . ."

Third conflict: But as he walks into the bedroom with the tea and flowers, Natasha glares at him. Before he can utter a word, she blurts out, "You're so selfish. I'm sorry I ever married you. Please go away and leave me alone." She refuses to talk to him and gives him the cold shoulder. As Boris walks out the door, he is stunned and confused that Natasha could refuse such kindness. She has just thrown a javelin through his heart, and he is bleeding badly. He prays, "Lord, what do I do now? I wasn't prepared for this."

His mind races for another weapon to pull out of his arsenal, but nothing he can think of seems appropriate for this battle so he grabs his Bible and begins prayerfully searching for appropriate passages to help him plan his next move. He begins reading Galatians 6:1: "Brethren, even if anyone is caught in any trespass, you who are spiritual, restore such a one in a spirit of gentleness; each one looking to yourself, so that you too will not be tempted." Boris prayerfully traces a string of 23 cross-references through the Bible. Little by little a new battle plan emerges.

He decides that he's going to write her a letter. "Natasha really loves for me to write her letters," he says to himself. "I'll assure her of my love, acknowledging any faults of which I'm aware, and let her know I'm willing to do whatever is biblically necessary to resolve this conflict. I'm also going to graciously remind her that as a Christian, she also has a responsibility to resolve this conflict biblically. I'll support my case with Scripture."

When he finishes the letter, Boris gently walks into the bedroom where Natasha is lying on the bed crying. He puts his arms around her, assures her of his love, gives her the letter, and tells her that he'll be waiting in the living room for her to finish resolving the conflict according to biblical principles, assuring her that he has every intention of also doing so. Then he walks out softly, leaving her to ponder his kindness in light of her sinful attitude. He is praying that as she reads the letter, sees and smells the flowers, remembers the chores he's done for her, the tea he's brought to her, and most of all the gentle spirit with which he's been imploring her to "repent," she will surrender.

Then, it happens. As he's sitting on the sofa in the living room praying for a resolution, he hears the door to the bedroom begin to open. In walks Natasha with tears in her eyes. She walks over to Boris, throws her arms around him, thanking him for responding so lovingly to her and asking him to forgive her for her sinful reactions. As he continues to talk, the conflict is brought to a biblical conclusion, and both walk away closer to each other and closer to the Lord.

Now, of course, the particular weapons Boris chose to use in this fictitious story will not be suited for every situation. But it should serve to provide you with some idea of the forethought, creativity, and patience that is usually necessary to overcome evil with good.

On the following page, there is a worksheet (which you may photocopy) to assist you in developing your own plan of attack as you by God's grace seek to overcome not only evil but also your own bitter feelings toward the one who has hurt you.

There is one final thought I would like to offer you. Suffering is part of the Christian life for which God has His own purposes. "Beloved, do not be surprised at the fiery ordeal among you, which comes upon you for your testing, as though some strange thing were happening to you" (1 Peter 4:12).

Sometimes that suffering comes at the hands of people we love and trust. I daresay that most of the wounds we experience as Christians are from friendly fire—they are inflicted by the hands of other Christians. One of God's purposes for such suffering is to conform us to His image that we might glorify Him, obtain eternal rewards, and learn how to live "the rest of the time in the flesh no longer for the lusts of men, but for the will of God" (1 Peter 4:2). God really will provide you with everything you need to become a *better* Christian rather than a *bitter* Christian as a result of being hurt. The choice is yours.

Overcoming Evil with Good Arsenal

Begin a list of the various ways you can "overcome evil with good" by responding to your offender in love when he or she sins against you in the future.

-

-

-

-

-

-

-

APPENDIX A:

Bitterness at God[1]

SOME PEOPLE—yes, even Christian people—become bitter at God. It's not that He has sinned against them and is in need of their forgiveness. It's a matter of their mishandling a difficult situation (a trial) that He has flung on them. By way of contrast, consider Job. In his trial, this blameless, upright, and God-fearing man didn't focus in on secondary causes—the Sabeans, the Chaldeans, the fire that fell from heaven, or the great wind that came from across the wilderness (cf. Job 1:14–19). Rather, he kept his eyes on the character of God, who for His own eternal purposes allows human suffering.

The Bible says that after losing almost everything he had:

> Job arose and tore his robe and shaved his head, and he fell to the ground and worshiped. He said, "Naked I came from my mother's womb, and naked I shall return there. The LORD gave and the LORD has taken away. Blessed be the name of the LORD." Through all this Job did not sin nor did he blame God. (Job 1:20–22)

1. Much of this appendix has been adapted from chapter 12 of my book *Picking Up the Pieces* (Phillipsburg, NJ: P&R, 2012).

When people are bitter at God, it is usually because of some kind of loss. It could be the loss of good health, of a loved one, of wealth, of reputation, or even of a dream. Before you read any further, ask yourself, "What is it (if anything) that I have lost in connection with my bitterness?" If we're not careful, such losses can overshadow our entire outlook and cause us to be overcome with sorrow.[2] And inordinate grieving can metastasize into bitterness.

"But at what point does grieving become inordinate?"

Before His death, Jesus gave His disciples some disturbing information. He told them not only that the days ahead would involve considerable difficulty, but that He would no longer be with them. For quite some time, these men had had a special relationship with the Lord and a very real hope that He would be establishing His kingdom on earth in the immediate future.

How did they respond when they realized their hopes were about to be dashed? Their hearts became filled with sorrow. "But because I have said these things to you, sorrow has *filled your heart*" (John 16:6). The word *filled* implies a kind of filling that is complete. It is to fill to a full measure—or, as we might say, to "fill to the brim." When something is filled that completely, there is room for nothing else. When a heart is filled with sorrow, the sorrow so completely occupies one's life that it displaces everything else.

Now, there's nothing wrong with a little bit of sorrow.[3] In fact, Jesus was "a man of sorrows and acquainted with grief" (Isa. 53:3). Yet He also had an abundance of peace, joy,

2. Bitterness is an indication of a temporal (earthly) value system. The things we lose that tempt us to bitterness would have lasted for only a short while. Yet the bitterness we allow in our hearts causes us to lose eternal rewards (see 1 Tim. 4:8).

3. Jesus said, "Blessed are they who mourn, for those shall be comforted" (Matt. 5:4).

and love. He was able to say such things as "My peace I give to you" (John 14:27), "These things I have spoken to you so that My joy may be in you, and that your joy may be made full" (John 15:11), and "As the Father has loved Me, I have also loved you; abide in My love" (John 15:9). So, a certain amount of sorrow may simultaneously abide with love, joy, and peace in one's heart.

Jesus never let His sorrow prevent Him from fulfilling any of His responsibilities. That is, He never allowed His sorrow to become so great that it totally shut Him down or caused Him to sin. He certainly didn't become bitter. Why? Because He saw God's purpose in His trial.

> Now My soul has become troubled; and what shall I say, "Father, save Me from this hour"? But for this purpose I came to this hour. (John 12:27)

In the garden of Gethsemane, Jesus told His disciples, "My soul is exceedingly sorrowful, even to death. Stay here and watch with Me" (Matt. 26:38). He then proceeded to pray so agonizingly that "His sweat became like drops of blood" (Luke 22:44). His disciples, on the other hand, had allowed their sorrow to keep them from fully discharging the responsibilities He had just given them.

> He came out and proceeded as was His custom to the Mount of Olives; and the disciples also followed Him. When He arrived at the place, He said to them, *"Pray that you may not enter into temptation."* And He withdrew from them about a stone's throw, and He knelt down and began to pray, saying, "Father, if You are willing, remove this cup from Me; yet not My will, but Yours be done." Now an angel from heaven appeared to Him, strengthening Him. And being in agony He was praying very fervently; and His sweat became like

41

drops of blood, falling down upon the ground. When He rose from prayer, He came to the disciples and found them *sleeping from sorrow*, and said to them, "Why are you sleeping? Get up and pray that you may not enter into temptation." (Luke 22:39–46)

The disciples were exhausted as a result of their sorrow. Yet Jesus admonished them for sleeping when they should have been praying and commanded them to get back to work. When we are faced with any loss, it is normal for us to grieve. As Solomon said, "Sorrow is better than laughter, for by a sad countenance the heart is made better" (Eccl. 7:3 NKJV).

The danger comes when we allow our grief to become so great that it overpowers other things in our lives that God says we ought not to let slip—not the least of which is worshiping Him with a heart of (not to mention "filled" with) thanksgiving. When experiencing heartaches, we can easily allow sorrow to fill our lives to such an extent that we stop thinking about those things that generate love, joy, peace, or any other element of the Spirit's fruit. Our sorrow must not quench the Spirit's work in our lives. We ought not to grieve so much that we stop fulfilling our biblical responsibilities. Rather than allowing our sorrow to control us, we should continue to be controlled by the Spirit. To be "filled with the Spirit" (Eph. 5:18) is to be *controlled* by the Spirit. To be filled with sorrow is to be *controlled* by sorrow.

"But what if I'm already there? What if I've allowed my heart to be filled, or almost filled, with sorrow to the point that I'm shutting down mentally and emotionally? What if I have already become bitter at God?"

Then by the Spirit's enabling power, you will have to work hard at getting your sorrow back down to a manageable level and any bitterness eradicated from your heart. First, confess your inordinate grieving and bitterness to God, asking Him to forgive you and to grant you the grace to change your sinful thoughts and ways. Then begin to formulate the kind of thoughts that will generate the right kinds of feelings. "Whatever is true, whatever is honorable, whatever is right, whatever is pure, whatever is lovely, whatever is of good repute, if there is any excellence and if anything worthy of praise, dwell on these things" (Phil. 4:8). Rather than thinking only of what you've lost, think about how God may be using your loss to benefit you. Rather than thinking about how miserable you are, ponder how you can make someone else happy. Rather than worrying about what will happen to you tomorrow, figure out how you can be a blessing to someone today. Instead of grumbling and complaining, praise God for all the things He has done for you.

And keep your eyes peeled for self-pity, as it often locks arms with bitterness. Recognizing self-pitying thoughts and replacing them with thoughts of gratitude toward God is another way to deal with your bitterness toward Him. Here are a few examples of how, by God's grace, you may turn your thoughts around.

> *Self-pitying thought*: "Why don't You love me as much as You love so-and-so?"
> *Grateful thought*: "Thank You for loving me even though my love for You is so feeble."

> *Self-pitying thought*: "Why did You allow such a hurtful thing to happen to me?"
> *Grateful thought*: "Thank You for Your loving faithfulness to me. Though I do not yet understand why this has happened, and can't even imagine how You intend to glorify Yourself through this loss or cause it to work together for my good, I will trust You."

Self-pitying thought: "All I ever wanted in life was to have _____. Why can't You let me have such a good thing?"

Grateful thought: "Thank You for giving me what I need (and not necessarily what I want). You know what is best for me. I know that You will withhold no good thing from those who walk uprightly."

Self-pitying thought: "I hate my life. I wish I'd never been born."

Grateful thought: "Thank You for the life You have given me. I know that the ultimate purpose for which I was created was to glorify You and enjoy You forever."

Self-pitying thought: "What's the use of trying to live the Christian life? It's too much trouble and will never pay enough dividends—at least not in this life."

Grateful thought: "Thank You that You have saved me, that no matter how difficult things get in my life, You 'will never leave me nor forsake me' and that I will spend eternity with You in a place where there is no more sin, or sickness, or suffering."

Remember that self-pity is rooted in such things as self-ishness, pride, idolatry, envy, and resentment. It tempts us to focus on what we don't have (selfishness), what we believe we deserve (pride), what we want (idolatry), what others have been given that we have not (envy), and why God has seen fit to bless others instead of us (resentment).

Another thing you can do to help get your sorrow under control (and to keep bitterness from reentering your heart) is to fulfill your biblical responsibilities. If you are not already doing so, get involved in ministering to others. Yes, you can do these things even though your heart is sorrowful. It may not be easy, and it probably won't be fun at first. But in time, your mind will be occupied with more noble thoughts than with what you have lost. The satisfaction that comes from being responsible and the joy that comes from serving others will begin to refill your heart as it displaces your superfluous grief.

So ultimately, the way to get any excessive sorrow in your heart back down to a manageable level is to do two things: think biblically and act biblically (responsibly).

Take a few minutes right now to make a list of any responsibilities you've been neglecting as a result of being consumed with your loss. Then write out Philippians 4:8. List those things you can meditate on (and thank God for) when you are tempted to think about all you've lost. (Perhaps the first entry should be "things to put on my Phillipians 4:8 list.") Put this list in your wallet or purse and carry it with you wherever you go. And the next time you catch yourself murmuring, complaining, or inordinately grieving over your loss, pull it out for a quick review. Then, set your mind on thinking or doing something more eternally significant than cultivating a root of bitterness toward the One who has redeemed you and fitted you for heaven.

APPENDIX B:

Loving Another from Afar[1]

MUCH OF WHAT we have been looking at in this booklet has to do with loving those who have offended us. Christians are commanded not only to love their neighbors, but also to love their enemies.

> You have heard that it was said, "*You shall love your neighbor and hate your enemy.*" But I say to you, love your enemies and pray for those who persecute you, so that you may be sons of your Father who is in heaven; for He causes His sun to rise on the evil and the good, and sends rain on the righteous and the unrighteous. (Matt. 5:43–45)

Sometimes, we are called to love others from afar. Ex-spouses, ex-fiancés and fiancées, ex-boyfriends and girlfriends, and malicious enemies (former friends) all may require a special kind of long-distance love. In other words, rather than loving up close and personal, you may have to learn how to love from a distance. Rather than thinking in terms of *external* manifestations of love (which you may have formerly been able to practice by virtue of the time you

---

1. This appendix has been adapted from chapter 5 of my book *Picking Up the Pieces* (Phillipsburg, NJ: P&R, 2012).

previously spent in the other person's presence), you will now have to think in terms of *internal* ones.

Manifestations of Love

"What do you mean by external and internal manifestations of love?"

External manifestations of love are those related to our words and actions. Internal manifestations of love are those related to our thoughts and motives. Look at the description of biblical love found in 1 Corinthians 13:4–7.

- Love is patient.
- Love is kind.
- Love is not jealous.
- Love does not brag.
- Love is not arrogant.
- Love does not act unbecomingly.
- Love does not seek its own.
- Love is not provoked.
- Love does not take into account a wrong suffered.
- Love does not rejoice in unrighteousness.
- Love rejoices in the truth.
- Love bears all things.
- Love believes all things.
- Love hopes all things.
- Love endures all things.

Each of these elements describes positive and negative[2] aspects of what love looks like. For the most part, they are

2. Implicit in each of the negative elements of love is its antithetical positive counterpart.

observable external behaviors (they are essentially verbs in the original[3]). But they describe something internal—an attitude of the heart that involves giving oneself unselfishly for the benefit of another.

Up to this point, you've had opportunity to demonstrate each of these elements of love to your offender in tangible ways. Now, you may have to learn how to love this person in absentia. What's more, to keep yourself free from bitterness, you will have to limit the amount of time you spend thinking about him. But when you do think of him be careful to control your thoughts, so that you will not allow yourself to develop other unloving attitudes (such as jealousy or contempt) that could result in unloving words or actions. If you change the content of your thought patterns, your love will take on a new form and your feelings will ultimately change for the better.

Consider for a moment God's love for us. Isn't His love sometimes manifested in forms that appear contradictory to each other? For example, sometimes His love is demonstrated when He does something special in answer to prayer that is "far more abundantly beyond all that we ask or think" (Eph. 3:20). At other times, His love takes on the form of a divine spanking: "For those whom the Lord loves He disciplines" (Heb. 12:6). These two manifestations of love may appear dissimilar on the surface, but when viewed from a biblical perspective, they are simply different forms of the same thing.

So it is with you. You can learn to love your offender in different ways. For instance, instead of fulfilling the "love is patient" clause by restraining your anger[4] should your

3. Biblical love involves motion (action) more than it does emotion.
4. The Greek word for *patience* has to do with being "long-tempered." We might say that a patient person has a long fuse instead of a short one. The patient person exercises self-control by restraining his angry passions, especially in stressful situations.

offender do something hurtful directly to you, you may now have to be patient by restraining your anger over the fact that your offender has not yet acknowledged how he has hurt you, or over the way he may be misrepresenting to others the exact nature of how your relationship has deteriorated.

As for the "love is kind" component, rather than simply showing kindness directly to your offender in word and deed when he is ill or irritable, you may now have to do so by saying kind things to others about him. You will need to be extra careful to avoid all elements of cruelty or harshness (two antitheses of kindness). And you will have to do so not only in any direct dealings with the offender, but also in your communications about him to others—especially to those who are not involved.

Let's jump down the list a bit to "love does not act unbecomingly."[5] This is the fourth in a list of eight consecutive negative aspects of love, each of which is intended to draw attention to its opposite. To act unbecomingly is to act in an ugly way or to do something that will later cause shame. When you were actively involved in a relationship with your offender, you were (presumably) careful not to say or do ugly, shameful things. You made a conscious effort to be honorable in all your dealings with him. You were polite, attentive, courteous, and considerate, used good manners, and were thoughtful of his needs and desires. You certainly avoided crude remarks, foul language, vitriolic comments, pejorative statements, selfish decisions, gossip, and slander.

At this juncture, you may not have as many opportunities to practice the positive side of this element. (Although, when

5. For an excellent treatment of all fifteen characteristics of 1 Corinthians 13 love in a brief package, see Jay E. Adams, "The Use of 1 Corinthians 13 in Counseling," in *Update on Christian Counseling*, vol. 2 (Phillipsburg, NJ: P&R Publishing, 1981), 35–48.

you are in the presence of your offender, you must continue to do constructive things as much as possible.) But you will have plenty of opportunity to practice not doing and saying shameful, destructive things to or about him. Moreover, you will almost certainly be more tempted to do and say these unbecoming things now that the relationship has changed. Perhaps you've already done some improper things since the offense occurred. Confess those to the Lord (if you haven't already done so). Ask His forgiveness as well as the forgiveness of those to whom you've said unloving things.

From now on, as much as is possible, commit yourself to doing and saying honorable things in reference to your offender. Of all the ways you may "love" the person at whom you've been bitter, from this point forward perhaps the two most important are to "think no evil" and "believe all things."

These elements are different sides (negative and positive) of the same coin. They have to do with the moment-by-moment decisions we make concerning the manner in which we think about the object of our love. To "think no evil" means not keeping a running list of wrongs the other person has committed against you. It's the result of overlooking someone's debt, of no longer holding a person's transgressions against him. Such "forgetfulness" is not forgetting in the sense of having amnesia,[6] but in refusing to call to mind that which has been forgiven.

To "believe all things" is to put the best possible interpretation on a person's behavior. Suppose your offender does something that could be viewed in ten different ways, nine of which are bad. Love will reject the nine and accept the one. In the *absence of hard evidence to the contrary*, love

---

6. God, who says, "I will not remember your sins" (Isa. 43:25), is omniscient and therefore cannot have amnesia.

will go out of its way (investing time, effort, and thought) to imagine a good interpretation of the matter before seriously considering a bad one. Love doesn't slam the gavel down on the judicial bench of its mind, declaring a person guilty without looking seriously at all the evidence (which, by the way, is often not readily available). Can you love your offender in this way? You can if you truly are a Christian who has been forgiven of your sins and had the love of God poured into your heart (Rom. 5:5).

I'd like to encourage you to begin making your own list of specific ways you can love your offender in absentia. The worksheet that follows (Appendix C) contains a partially completed list of specific ways a person may demonstrate all fifteen elements of 1 Corinthians 13 love to a former boyfriend, girlfriend, fiancé/fiancée, spouse, or friend. The inventory is incomplete because it is designed to be personalized to your own particular set of circumstances.

APPENDIX C:

Loving "in Absentia" Worksheet[1]

IN 1 CORINTHIANS 13, we find a description of what love *does*. As we have seen from the biblical perspective, love is more of a verb than a noun. There are fifteen descriptive verbs about love found in verses 4–7 of this famous "love chapter."[2] Eight of the fifteen are stated negatively (love is *not*/does *not* . . .); seven are stated positively (love is/does . . .). The negative descriptions imply their positive counterparts as the positive descriptions imply their negative counterparts (lack of love). In other words, being patient with someone means that you will not be impatient, and "not seeking its own" implies that love will seek the interests of the person who is being loved. Since you, for the most part, will be loving your offender "in absentia," you will usually find yourself loving him more through the negative means than through the positive ones.

Listed below are seventy-four specific things you may still be able to do (or not do) for your offender as an expression of biblical love. They are categorized under the fifteen ele-

1. This appendix has been adapted from Appendix E of my book *Picking Up the Pieces* (Phillipsburg, NJ: P&R, 2012).

2. The list is sufficient but not exhaustive. There are other aspects of biblical love found elsewhere in the Bible that are not mentioned here (e.g., "love is not fearful," 1 John 4:18).

ments of love. Depending on your exact set of circumstances, some of these suggestions will be unfeasible, impractical, or impossible to accomplish. In certain cases, and with certain individuals, it may even be unwise (if not dangerous) to attempt them. But perhaps there are a few items on the list that you've not yet considered for your unique situation. So, there is a space for you to add some of your own applications for each facet of love.

Love Is Patient

- I will not lose my temper (have a short fuse) when my offender doesn't _____.
- I will be forbearing with my offender's foibles and idiosyncratic behaviors.
- I will restrain my angry words and actions when my offender does something selfish.
- I will not write off my offender if he doesn't immediately see things from my point of view.
- I will continue to pray for my offender's bad attitudes until the Lord changes them (or until He changes my ability to handle them more biblically).

- _____.

- _____.

Love Is Kind

- I will say kind things about my offender.
- I will offer to run errands for my offender.
- I will express sympathy and concern to my offender when he is in the midst of trouble (rather than gloating that he is finally getting what he deserves).

- I will be considerate of how my decisions will affect my offender. (I will not ignore my offender's interests or feelings.)
- I will not be excessively passive toward my offender but will actively look for God-honoring ways to be a blessing to him.
- I will not be cruel or malicious to my offender.

- _____.

- _____.

Love Is Not Jealous

- I will not become resentful if God sees fit to bless my offender with the things for which I am longing.
- I will rejoice in God's goodness toward my offender, remembering that it was the goodness of God that led me to repentance (cf. Rom. 2:4).
- I will offer to share something I have with my offender.
- I will pray that my offender will succeed in a particular area of his interest.
- I will not allow myself to focus on what I have lost as a result of being offended, but will rather consider how the Lord may use the offense for good in both of our lives.

- _____.

- _____.

Love Does Not Brag

- I will not inordinately seek my offender's approval.
- I will not put my offender down in order to make myself look good.

- I will not brag about the achievements God has wrought in my life since the offense occurred.
- I will acknowledge to others my own sinful contributions to the breakdown of my relationship with the offender.
- I will not play the martyr (or the victim).
- If I boast about anything to those who are aware of the offense, it will be about how God is using it to make me more like Christ.
- _____.
- _____.

Love Is Not Arrogant

- I will ask my offender for advice from time to time.
- When my offender reproves or criticizes me, I will not get defensive but will acknowledge my faults and if necessary ask for his forgiveness.
- I will not make unfair or unrealistic demands on my offender.
- I will not make my offender grovel for my forgiveness. ("You haven't offended any ol' body, you offended me . . . .")
- I will be grateful for any kindness my offender may show to me.
- I will pray that my offender's relationship with the Lord will be restored more than I will pray that his relationship with me will be restored.
- I will guard my heart against having a critical, censorious, condemning attitude toward my offender.
- _____.
- _____.

Love Does Not Act Unbecomingly

- I will make every effort to be courteous to my offender whenever I am in his presence.
- I will not say or do anything to disgrace or embarrass my offender.
- I will be a good Christian example for my offender.
- I will not gossip about or slander my offender to others.
- I will not resort to sarcastic, profane, condescending, or disrespectful forms of communication, but will seek to build up (edify) my offender whenever appropriate.
- _____.
- _____.

Love Does Not Seek Its Own

- I will not manipulate my offender.
- I will not try to make my offender jealous.
- Whenever I have opportunities to show love to my offender, I will examine my motives to be sure I'm not giving (meeting his needs) in order to get something back.
- I will not waste time dwelling on how my offender doesn't love me or appreciate me.
- I will not allow fear of what my offender might take from me to prevent me from seeing (and perhaps meeting) his needs.
- I will not superimpose my will for my offender over God's will for him.
- _____.
- _____.

Love Is Not Provoked

- I will not talk to my offender when I'm upset with him but will wait until my anger is under control.
- I will remind myself from time to time about my offender's good qualities.
- I will think before I speak to my offender when he does or says something to push my buttons.

- _____.

- _____.

Love Does Not Take into Account a Wrong Suffered

- I will forgive my offender (either verbally or in my heart) for every hurtful thing he has done to me.
- I will not bear a grudge against my offender.
- I will not review in my mind the hurtful things my offender did to me during our relationship.
- I will not try to console myself by talking to others about my offender's faults.

- _____.

- _____.

Love Does Not Rejoice in Unrighteousness[3]

- I will not take pleasure in any foolish decisions that I learn my offender has made.
- I will not take pleasure in any hurtful things others do to my offender.

3. It should be noted that "not rejoicing in unrighteousness" carries with it the responsibility of clearing one's conscience of offenses committed against an offender in the past (cf. Prov. 28:13; Acts 24:16; 1 Tim. 1:18–19). For more information on how to do this, see my recording "How to Clear Your Conscience," available from www.Loupriolo.com or www.Soundword.com.

- I will not take pleasure in any injustice that befalls my offender.
- I will not take pleasure in any acts of vengeance against my offender that my sinful heart may imagine.
- I will not take pleasure in any thought of others' sinning against my offender.
-     _____.
-     _____.

Love Rejoices in the Truth

- I will not be unfair when dealing with my offender, but will treat him with justice and equity.
- I will not unfairly side with others against my offender, but will defend him against any false accusations.
- I will not allow my mind to fantasize about things involving my offender that either are sinful or do not conform to reality.
-     _____.
-     _____.

Love Bears All Things

- I will not view this offense as something intolerable, unbearable, or beyond my ability to handle as a Christian.
- I will not take personally every offense my offender commits against me in the future.
- I will make every effort to patiently put up with my offender's sins, foibles, and idiosyncrasies.

- I will make every effort to cover[4] my offender's sins (and failures) with love.

- _____ .

- _____ .

Love Believes All Things

- I will not be unduly suspicious of my offender.
- I will make it a point to put the best interpretation on my offender's behavior unless I have hard evidence to the contrary.
- I will not jump to hasty and unfounded conclusions about my offender.
- I will not judge my offender's motives.
- I will not criticize my offender if he does something that the Bible does not say is sinful.

- _____ .

- _____ .

Love Hopes All Things

- I will pray regularly for my offender.
- I will not waste time trying to figure out all that is wrong in (or what can go wrong in) my offender's life.
- I will look for ways that God may be working through the offense for His glory.
- I will look for ways that God may be working for the good of my offender.
- I will look for opportunities to give biblical hope to my offender.

4. This phrase in verse 7 of 1 Corinthians 13 may also rightly be translated "love covers all things."

- I will choose to believe that God is working all things together for the good of those who love Him and are called according to His purpose and that someday (in this life or the next) I will see exactly how He has done so.

- _____.

- _____.

Love Endures All Things

- I will not allow his offense to keep me from fulfilling my biblical responsibilities toward my offender.
- I will commit myself to maintaining Christlike attitudes toward my offender.
- I will not allow the wrong my offender has done to cause me to conclude that he is beyond God's ability to save or restore.
- I will remind myself often that suffering is a part of the Christian life and thank God that He has seen fit to use my offender to the end that I may become more like the Lord Jesus Christ.

- _____.

- _____.